The Republic of Paraguay

1. Introduction

General Alfredo Stroessner came to power following a successful coup in 1954. His military dictatorship has since then been "legitimized" by controlled periodic general elections, and the constitution has been amended to permit his constant re-election. Although President Stroessner permits a very limited formal opposition, he can arbitrarily suppress any individual opponent or political group, either on a temporary or long term basis.

Accurate and up to date information on Paraguay is difficult to obtain. It is one of the most isolated countries in South America and the international media seem to have little interest in it. But the opposition press has at times managed to report flagrant violations of human rights. Exile sources also provide important data on occasion. Amnesty International reports in 1966 and 1971 confirmed a continuing level of repression, which appears to have been maintained up to the present.

The facade of legality which the regime presents has little relevance to the actual situation of human rights in Paraguay. The emphasis of this report, therefore, will be on the illegal procedures it employs. In this context, the analysis will focus on the following issues of particular concern to AI:

(a) wide-scale arrests or disappearances of suspected political opponents and/or their relatives;
(b) long term detention without trial;
(c) the use of torture.

2. Legal Situation

In evaluating the human rights situation in Paraguay, it is necessary to draw a distinction between the safeguards enshrined in the constitution and the reality of political repression.

The 1967 constitution provides the classic safeguards against violations of human rights. For instance, article 50 guarantees the freedom of the individual, article 56 freedom of movement, article 59 forbids detention without charge for more than 24 hours and article 65 outlaws torture and maltreatment. Other articles provide for the inviolability of residence (article 68), the inviolability of private correspondence (69), freedom of association (76) and *habeas corpus* (78).

However much of the spirit of the constitution has been eroded by laws that allow the executive to restrict any opposition activity considered to be of a "subversive" character. The Law for the Defence of Public Peace and Liberty of Persons condemns, "whosoever publicly preaches hate between Paraguayans or the destruction of social classes" (1-6 year prison sentence), illegal organization (3-6 years) and those who are members of or affiliated to any Communist Party or organization that proposes "to destroy violently the republican and democratic regime of the nation" (3-5 years).

According to the interpretation of the Supreme Court of Justice, all individual rights may be suppressed if a state of emergency is declared. President Stroessner had proclaimed states of emergency at three-monthly intervals since 1954, lifting it only on election days, and alleging the threat of communist subversion. Article 79 of the 1967 constitution provides for the declaration of a state of emergency only "in defence of the Constitution" and "in cases of international war or conflict, foreign invasion, internal turmoil or a grevious threat to one of them". This was intended as an extraordinary measure, but it has continued for 22 years, although the president himself has repeatedly claimed that the country has preserved internal peace better than any other on the continent.

While legal provisions for the trial of "subversives" exist, the paradox lies in the fact that political prisoners are only rarely charged or sentenced. Paraguayan exiles have alleged that the executive ignores legal safeguards and interprets legislation capriciously. Political trials occasionally occur – as for instance the trial early in 1976 of 13 prisoners detained after an alleged coup attempt in November 1974. Such trials, however, remain the exception rather than the rule, and there is no guarantee that convicted prisoners will be released on completion of their sentences. Arbitrary arrest, kidnapping (both within Paraguay and in neighbouring states), incommunicado detention, and refusal to provide relatives of prisoners with information concerning their arrests, form the pattern of political imprisonment in Paraguay. It is within this context that the government's tolerance of limited press freedom and opposition activity must be seen. The government possesses the additional sanction of threatening even the circumscribed freedoms which remain.

3. Number of Prisoners

Political prisoner figures can only be estimates: it is difficult to calculate the number of families unwilling to report an arrest for fear of reprisals, the number of "disappeared" persons whose detention is not confirmed and the political prisoners scattered in small groups over a large number of police stations, some in the countryside. Furthermore, the government does not acknowledge the existence of political prisoners as distinct from criminals. Nevertheless, estimates from various sources over the years have been fairly consistent:

Year	*Estimated Number of Political Detainees*	*Source*
1966	100-250	Amnesty International (Report on Paraguay).
1970	300	*La Razôn*, Buenos Aires, 16 October 1970.
1971	100	*The Guardian*, London, 19 October 1971.
1972	250	Amnesty International document (including a list of 95 names).

1973	300	*Prensa Latina,* Feature Service, 15 February 1973 (list of 83 names known to AI).
1975	338	*Agencia Noticiosa Paraguaya,* Buenos Aires, 23 June 1975.
Early 1976	450	Amnesty International estimate (including list of 233 names).

One should differentiate between long term prisoners and those who are detained for less than a year. *Agencia Noticiosa Paraguaya* on 23 June 1975 listed three political prisoners in jail for 18 years (since 1958), five for 15 years, 30 for between 8 and 12 years and some 300 for over 9 months. At the same time, a team of the International Committee of the Red Cross, after visiting several places of detention, reported meeting 64 political prisoners *(International Review of the Red Cross,* number 172, July 1975).

Waves of arrests periodically enlarge the prison population for short periods. Some examples:

–February 1974, when large numbers of peasants and students were arrested;
–October 1974, when 120 peasants, members of the *Ligas Agrarias* (Agrarian –Leagues) were detained;
–November 1974 to January 1975, when 800 to 1,200 persons, many from the armed forces and the ruling *Colorado* Party were arrested for alleged involvement in a coup attempt;
–December 1975, when some 200 individuals were arrested, including approximately 100 suspected of Communist Party affiliation, five members of the *Marandu* Indian aid project and Liberal Radical Party members;
–April 1976, when about 350 persons were detained, including peasants and active members of the Roman Catholic Church.

There are, therefore, massive short term arrests in situations which the government considers to be threatening. This is frequently an anticipatory move by the authorities to crush, at basic organizational level, any potential risk. Long term imprisonment on the other hand, is used by the authorities as a warning to all citizens that political transgressors (notably communists) risk life imprisonment without trial.

4. Analysis of Prisoners

AI's files contain the names of 233 known political prisoners: 205 men and 28 women. AI's list includes 29 students, 27 workers of various kinds, 11 teachers and academics, 10 farmers or peasants, 10 small traders or artisans, 10 lawyers or members of the professions, and smaller numbers of writers, journalists, military personnel, policemen, housewives and artists. Although AI's information relating to individual prisoners is incomplete, it would appear that most long term prisoners are from urban areas. There appears to be a much wider range of ages among Paraguayan political prisoners than in most other Latin American countries, where the majority tend to be young.

Any analysis of the relatively small number of long term prisoners must take into account the significant proportion who are probably in prison by accident, rather than as a result of any political act. This category includes not only relatives punished instead of, or in addition to, the real activist, but also persons faced with long imprisonment through mistaken identity or false accusations.

Genuine political prisoners can be divided broadly into four main categories:

(a) *Members of the ruling Colorado Party and the military elite*
These include individuals purged as "problematic elements" or suspected of planning the overthrow of President Stroessner. Middle-ranking officers and militants of the ruling *Colorado* Party may be held for a number of years, while more prominent figures may secure their own release after a short period by renewed avowals of loyalty, or by deportation. Such prisoners are less likely to suffer the extremes of repression than are other political prisoners.

(b) *Members of the opposition parties*
This category consists mainly of members of the *Partido Revolucionario Febrerista, Partido Liberal Radical, Movimiento Popular Colorado, Partido Democrata Cristiano*, and usually involves the intelligentsia (lawyers, journalists, university professors and students, artists, professionals, etc). Arrest is generally the result of denunciations of the abuses of the government and demands for greater respect for human rights. The limits of permissible political criticism are unclear. These persons may find themselves arrested for actions which they had considered "safe", while at other times the risk of imprisonment might be foreseen. In general, imprisonment of this kind is temporary. In February 1975, the Liberal Radical Party reported that only two of its members were still in prison. This position was probably the same for all opposition parties, except the Communist Party.

(c) *Members of the Communist Party*
The Communist Party, which is proscribed, consists mainly of intellectuals and urban workers. Generally they have not been involved in revolutionary activities, but rather in basic attempts to organize. Nevertheless, communists have been so systematically persecuted that they have virtually never had the opportunity to function effectively as a party in Paraguay.

Three Communist Party leaders have been in prison since 1958, charged under the Law in Defence of Democracy (number 294). The three, Alfredo Alcorta, Julio Romas and Antonio Maidana, were all members of the central committee of the party. All three should have been released by 1961, but they remain in detention. The Inter-American Commission on Human Rights of the Organization of American States decided in April 1973 to request the release of Antonio Maidana and in October 1973 to request the release of Julio Rojas. Paraguay has not complied with either request.

This form of prolonged imprisonment serves as a threat and deterrent to other communist activists. Nonetheless, the Communist

Party did begin to recover some ground, with the clandestine return fron exile of its leaders. But the authorities immediately carried out large scale arrests inside the country and arranged for the abduction and return of activists in Argentina. In this way, approximately 100 members were arrested in raids at the end of 1975, including the secretary general of the party, Miguel Angel Soler, who subsequently disappeared.

(d) *Agrarian Prisoners*

This category includes organized peasants, mostly *mestizos* (of mixed Spanish and Guarani Indian origin–the majority of the population). It also includes individuals working with such peasants, for instance, priests and social scientists–Paraguayan and foreign. Such prisoners may be arrested for short terms to prevent their participation in aid schemes which are deemed subversive, although the schemes are organized on a communal rather than a political basis. Such was the case of Father Braulio Maciel, who was arrested with other members of the Jejui agricultural experiment in 1975 and released after a few months' detention.

Since 1968, the Roman Catholic Church has, through its work with the large and impoverished rural population, become gradually more involved in social change by non-violent means. The ruling elite has shown disquiet at this development: any change in the condition of the rural population might loosen present patterns of political loyalty, which ensure acceptance of the status quo by this large sector. The authorities therefore tend to denounce church-backed rural projects as "collectivist experiments" or as "communist inflitration" into the church. However, the prestige of the church in rural areas has ensured that attacks on such projects are sporadic. But the occasional harassment apparently continues in the hope that this might eventually discourage all such programs.

One of the most brutal attacks on the *Ligas Agrarias* (Agrarian Leagues) took place at the *Colonia de San Isidro de Jejui* in February 1975. In this project, the impoverished Guarani Indians were leaving the unprofitable *minifundio* (smallholding) system of agriculture to exploit new, uncultivated forest lands on a communal working basis and to create consumer cooperatives. On 8 February 1975, the army and police raided the hamlet of Jejui at night. Hundreds of peasants were shot or arrested and the foreign priests involved in the project were deported. Houses were ransacked and confiscations included books, Bibles and religious notes copied out by the peasants. Some 90,000 guaranies (US $12,500), donated by European charitable agencies for the purchase of land, disappeared. The Christian community of Jejui remained under military surveillance until at least the end of 1975.

Further cases of official devastation of peasant villages have been reported in the regions of Buena Vista, Colonia Oviedo, Pilar, Cordillera, Santa Rosa and Tacuati. More recently, five members of the

Marandu (Guarani for "message") Project–an Indian aid/information agency attached to the Catholic University of Asunción–were arrested and reportedly tortured at the end of November and the beginning of December 1975. They included the eminent anthropologist and director of the project, Professor Miguel Chase-Sardi, and Professor Mauricio Schwartzman, a sociologist at the Catholic University. The *Marandu* Project included courses about legal rights, cooperatives, health and diet and conditions of employment. It encouraged efforts by the Indians themselves to organize in order to improve their living conditions–which at present are extremely bad.

5. Location of Prisons

There do not appear to be centers specifically for the detention of political prisoners in Paraguay. The majority of those who remain in prison for more than a year are held in small numbers in *comisarías* (local police stations), sharing one or more of the few small cells available.

Although there are occasional reports of prisoners being held in provincial *comisarías,* the majority of known cases are detained in the capital, Asunción. This may be due to the fact that the detention of provincial peasants could pass unnoticed by human rights advocates in the capital. It is also possible that security reasons require the transfer to Asunción, for interrogation and long term imprisonment, of persons originally arrested and detained in the countryside.

In the capital, the *comisarías* known to hold male political prisoners are numbers One, Three, Four, Seven, Eight, Nine and 11. The Central Department of Investigations, at the police headquarters in Asunción, directs activities against political opponents of the regime. The principal Asunción prisons are situated in the suburb of Tacumbu. They consist of the National Penitentiary (occupied mainly by convicted criminals) and the *Batallon de Seguridad* (Security Battallion)–where political prisoners are held usually for short terms, prior to release or transfer to *comisarías.* The *Batallon de Seguridad* is also used as a forced labour camp for large numbers of prisoners (reportedly more than 1,000), particularly following the sporadic waves of mass detentions.

Another prison, *Peña Hermosa,* is situated on an island in the Paraguay River. Political prisoners were held there in the mid-1960s, but it is not known whether this prison is still used for political detentions.

The two women's detention centers, *Comisaría de Fernando de la Mora* and *Comisaría de Santisima Trinidad* (both near Asunción), hold female political prisoners who have spent more than 7 years in prison. They may share cells with prostitutes and are subjected to abuse by the local policemen. Many of them are relatives of political dissidents. Relatives are taken as "hostages" pending the appearance of the wanted dissident, or as a punishment for the activities of the latter, or to ensure their silence following the assassination of a male relative.

6. Prison Conditions

Prison conditions have improved to some extent following publicity in 1974 by the Paraguayan Human Rights Commission and before the subsequent visits of representatives of the International Committee of the Red Cross.

As political prisoners tend to be distributed in small groups among various *comisarías*, conditions vary according to such arbitrary factors as the personality of the *comisario* (police chief), the inclinations of the jailers or the prisoner's economic and family status. However, the following are typical features of prison life:

(a) *Overcrowding*
The number of prisoners in each cell varies, but overcrowding is common. Prisoners often have to take turns to sleep because there may not be enough room for all to lie down. Personal belongings are hung from the roof to save space.

(b) *Bad hygenic conditions*
Cells frequently lack any ventilation. There may be no toilets available, only small tins. As these are only changed every few days, the resultant stench is appalling.

(c) *Maltreatment*
As well as the occasional beatings, some *comisarías* apparently practice continuous maltreatment. There are reports that prisoners in *Comisaría* Number One have been confined by ankle chains which severely restrict movement. Other disciplines include forcing prisoners to carry pails of excrement between the latrine and the cesspool during the hours of darkness and ice-cold baths outdoors during the cold season. In *Comisaría* Number Four, cell doors and bars are electrified to prevent escape attempts.

(d) *Malnutrition*
Food is scarce and of little nutritional value. Often corrupt officials intercept even the meagre meat rations allocated and family food parcels before they reach prisoners. The daily meal that relatives are allowed to provide is often all that enables prisoners to survive hunger and malnutrition. However, this assistance is not available for many detainees from the provinces or who are of poor origin.

(e) *Family Visits*
Family visits depend very much on the political situation and the good will of the *comisario.* On average there may be one weekly visit of three to five minutes by one relative, in the presence of a number of policemen. There are cases of prisoners remaining absolutely incommunicado for long periods of time, and other cases of prisoners being allowed to meet relatives for up to half an hour.

(f) *Facilities*
It is unusual for prisoners to be allowed reading material. They are not clothed to meet the extremes of Paraguay's tropical climate (short but cold winters and very hot and humid summers). With the other

deprivations, this can cause endemic ill health (tuberculosis, asthma, etc) on a large scale. Some prisoners become chronically sick, physically and mentally. In the Tacumbu camp, work, which consists of breaking stones or making bricks, is compulsory for 12 to 15 hours a day, including Sundays and public holidays. Prisoners live in huts, sleeping and eating on the floor, and are fed on a starvation diet. Beatings are frequent, but there is no medical attention.

7. Torture Allegations

Torture in Paraguay has been condemned both by specialized international organizations and by the country's Roman Catholic Church, which has denounced the torture of prisoners, including priests. Following an abortive coup in November 1974, it was reported that "hundreds of officials had been questioned under torture". Although the use of torture appears to be general, it is not necessarily applied systematically. It may depend on the place and length of detention and the personality of the jailers involved. It is generally true that political prisoners are subjected to torture in the first stages of interrogation, which usually takes place in the *Departamento de Delitos y Vigilancia* (Department of Offences and Vigilance) of the Ministry of Internal Affairs or at *Comisaría* Number Three.

It is not clear what purpose such torture serves, since the extraction of false confessions does not seem relevant, as political prisoners are rarely brought to trial. Torture may, however, be seen as a means of persuading other detainees to disclose names and information concerning potential or real opponents of the regime. It has been argued that torture is applied primarily as a punishment for and deterrent to opposition activities. The use of torture as a form of punishment is confirmed by the fact that after interrogation and the transfer of the prisoner to a long term detention cell, regular maltreatment is likely to continue throughout the period of detention. The extent varies with the type of prisoner and the inclinations of the jailer.

Methods of torture mentioned in allegations include:

- *el sargento* (the sergeant), a cat-of-nine-tails with lead balls at the tip of each thong;
- submersion to the point of near drowning in a bath of water or human excrement;
- application of electric shock to sensitive parts of the body;
- prolonged beating with clubs and whips;
- burning sensitive parts of the body with cigarettes and hot iron bars.

A typical example of such treatment is provided in the following testimony from a prisoner released in 1972 after 8 years in prison:

> On arrest I was beaten, then taken to the investigations department where I underwent hideous tortures throughout the day from rubber truncheons with which they hit me on the soles of my feet, and all over my body including my head.
>
> . . .The police call this beating "softening up", in other words, the first stage of the torture process. Afterwards comes the electric prod and "the

pinchers", which consists in crushing the fingernails with this instrument. Finally, there is the famous "bath", which is a family-size washing basin, filled with water, urine and human excrement. They tied my hands and feet, then they pushed me under the water, at the same time squeezing my testicles. When I ran out of breath, I began to swallow the filthy water full of urine and excrement. They pulled me out of the bath half dead to make me do physical exercises, so as to expel all the water which I had swallowed and also to give me back my strength. Once the torturers see that one is in a condition to put up with more torture, they put you under the water again. They tortured me in this way for two nights running. . .

When I was detained in the *Comisaría* Number One. . . I suffered constant torture, including being chained all together with 10 companions. . . We were kept in that state for two years, tied by both legs, without being able to move at all, except to sit and lie down. The torment did not stop there, since, whilst so chained, we were beaten with rubber truncheons and swords, and, in order to get in good favour with their superiors they stood and walked on top of our bodies.

Other reports cite the case of a 20-year old pregnant woman who, after three days of continuous torture, leading to a haemorrhage, was released "because there was no sufficient cause for maintaining her detention". There are also reports of children, some less than 10 years old, being tortured in *Comisaría* Number Two for alleged petty theft.

There has been confirmation from several sources that, in the past, the security forces of President Stroessner received some form of training from foreign sources (including former Nazi and SS members who escaped from Europe after World War II. It has also been reported that Dr Josef Mengele, a former Nazi physician, was acting as an adviser as late as 1971). More recently, specialists attached to the United States Central Intelligence Agency (CIA) have been accused of training Paraguayans in modern psychological methods of interrogation, including the use of drugs.

8. Released Prisoners

Although article 149 of the Paraguayan constitution provides congress with the right to declare an amnesty for any type of prisoner, and article 180 allows the president to commute sentences, these clauses have never been used. Any public appeal for an amnesty usually meets with strong governmental disapproval. Few such appeals in the past 20 years have escaped retaliation, the exception being a public meeting organized by the Liberal Radical Party in March 1975 and repeated appeals from dignatories of the Roman Catholic Church.

Releases tend to be as arbitrary as arrests. Some patterns can be discerned however: long term prisoners are sometimes released in old age, by which time their health is usually poor (as in the case of 70-year old Cristobal Valenzuela Ocampo, released in 1973 after 10 years' untried detention). In pre-electoral periods, some prisoners may be released (25 were freed prior to the 1973 elections) as a political gesture.

Released prisoners are often deported to neighbouring countries: to remain in (or to return to) Paraguay invites future re-arrest, or disappearance. As release is not assured by any formal procedures, this adds to the uncertainty in which prisoners and ex-prisoners live.

9. Capital Punishment–Political Executions

Capital punishment is less a threat to the lives of political opponents of the government than unofficial execution or death by "accident". These have accounted for a considerable number of victims over the years.

Article 25 of the constitution establishes that: "In no case shall the death penalty or the confiscation of property be applied for political considerations." In addition to this provision there is in fact virtually no death penalty in Paraguay for murder or other criminal offences. According to an AI report on prison conditions in Paraguay in 1966: "The last execution carried out upon a murderer convicted by a civil court was before the Second World War and long before General Stroessner came to power, and only one death sentence passed by a military court has been carried out in recent years."

However, as in other areas, there is a marked difference between legal provision and political reality.

(a) There have been cases of groups of communists (five members of the youth organization in 1965), *guerrilleros* (1966/67) and other political opponents (1974, 1975) who, following imprisonment and torture, have been found dead in the Paraguay River. When opponents of the government "disappear", it is possible that they may have been killed–this is at least as likely as their incommunicado detention.

(b) The uncontrolled used of torture sometimes leads to death. Following one of the largest waves of arrest (of some 800 persons allegedly involved in an attempted coup in November 1974), a Paraguayan exile source reported that an officer of the army, Beneficio López Quinoñez, died under torture. According to the same source, in addition to López Quinoñez (whose death was confirmed by the authorities), 10 other prisoners died in the weeks following the event. In April 1976, further cases of deaths under torture were reported.

(c) Cases of assassination have been explained by the authorities as prisoners' casualities suffered during an unsuccessful armed attack on the *comisaría.* Another variant of this is illustrated by the case of Commander Benitez Armoa, reportedly "shot while trying to escape". In fact, he was killed by other policemen so that he could not reveal the names of officers involved in the attempted coup of November 1974.

10. Amnesty International Action

AI has continuously expressed its concern about the situation of political prisoners in Paraguay. On many occasions it has appealed to President Stroessner on their behalf. Urgent action campaigns are launched whenever AI receives information about arrests that in most cases will be followed by torture. AI news releases have drawn international attention to reports of gross violations of human rights in Paraguay. For example, early in 1976, AI issued a news release denouncing the mass arrests which took place at the end of 1975. At the same time AI submitted a list of 55 arrests or disappearances to the Inter-American Commission on Human Rights of the Organization of American States, for investigation.

In May 1974, an AI mission (composed of Dr Horst Woesner, Judge of the Supreme Court of the Federal Republic of Germany, and Inger Fahlander of AI's International Secretariat) visited Paraguay. Their findings confirmed the continuing existence of long term imprisonment without trial and flagrant disregard of basic legal rights for alleged political offences.

At the beginning of 1976, AI had 59 Paraguayan cases under adoption or investigation, and approximately 30 further cases were being considered for future adoption or investigation.

Another aspect of AI's work—an important one in the case of Paraguay—has been the provision of relief to families of prisoners of conscience. This material humanitarian aid is particularly valuable as poverty is widespread in Paraguay: the imprisonment or disappearance of the breadwinner can mean destitution for the whole family.

11. Other Violations of Human Rights

Apart from the question of political imprisonment, disappearances and torture, human rights restrictions can be found in nearly all fields of social and political life.

(a) *Press Restrictions*

In December 1975 the International Press Institute described the press "virtually non-existent" in Paraguay. The opposition press is restricted to publications related to the Liberal Radical Party and Roman Catholic circles. Editorials or news items displeasing to the government frequently lead to the arrest of editors. For example members of the Liberal Radical Party directorate who were deemed responsible for the party organ *El Radical* are at present the subject of court proceedings. The offending newspaper was temporarily closed, only being allowed to resume publication in March 1976.

Official censorship is supplemented by "auto-censorship' , exercised by the "independent" newspapers *ABC Color* and *La Tribuna* to ensure their continued publication. In December 1974 the then editor of *ABC Color*, Roberto Thompson, was imprisoned for 4 months on charges of publishing "negative reports that disturb the peace".

(b) *Restrictions on Academic Life*

Freedom of thought is precluded by a complete ban on the introduction of any Marxist ideologies and the barring of leftwing teaching staff in the country's universities, where the student bodies are known to be infiltrated by police informers. Recent attempts by the government to manipulate student elections and control the Federation of Paraguayan Students (FUP) led to the formation of an independent student body. Government interventions at institutions of higher learning are frequent, the most recent example being a raid on the Jesuit Cristo Rey School in January 1976. Dissident professors may find themselves expelled, as happened recently to Liberal Radical leader Domingo Laino, who was considered to be Marxist-Leninist by a government-controlled student assembly of the Villarica branch of the Catholic University.

(c) *Trade Union Restrictions*
The Paraguayan Confederation of Workers, the main trade union body, is thought to be controlled by the government. Many democratic trade unionists have been imprisoned for periods of years. Attempts to organize Christian workers' organizations have been continuously obstructed by the government. Even organization on a local level has led to the imprisonment of workers, as happened early in 1976 at the important meat-processing plant of the Liebig company.

(d) *Judicial Partiality*
The majority of the Supreme Court members belong to the ruling *Colorado* Party and are appointed by the president. The impartiality of this body is therefore in doubt. Miscarriages of justice have been known to occur in criminal and civil as well as political cases. *Habeas corpus,* for instance, is automatically refused by a most singular interpretation of priorities of the constitutional clauses. The only case in the last 20 years in which *habeas corpus* was rejected by a majority of the judges and not unanimously related to the arrest of Liberal Radical leader Efren Gonzalez. The one dissenting voter was dismissed because he disobeyed the explicit instructions of the executive power, and was reportedly severely sanctioned by the ruling party, to which he belonged.

(e) *Harassment of Human Rights Activists*
The few individuals who dare to condemn human rights violations publicly or to assist political prisoners and their families are themselves at risk. Carmen Lara Castro, a Liberal Radical Party member of Congress and president of the Human Rights Commission has suffered imprisonment. Her husband has also been imprisoned and her son tortured. Possibly the best known case concerns Professor Luis Alfonso Resck, a moderate Christian Democrat Party leader, who regularly denounced arbitrary abuses. In January 1975 he was released from his 100th period of detention. These periods varied from a few hours to a few months, including confinement to isolated villages, and there were periods of torture. In his own words, "constitutional rights are violated here not only on paper but in the flesh".

(f) *Travel Restrictions*
A more recent violation of human rights is the refusal to grant passport

practice of keeping political prisoners at local police stations where conditions were generally poor.

There were misgivings at first among the families of political prisoners transferred to Emboscada that conditions would be harsher than in the capital, but, in fact, there have been improvements. Families are now allowed to visit inmates for about an hour once a week, whereas in the police stations prisoners were either held incommunicado or only permitted to be with family and friends for 15 minutes a week. Diet leaves much to be desired, although families and volunteers are allowed to provide prisoners with limited amounts of extra food, medicine and clothing. Several complaints have been submitted to the Minister of the Interior about the strict conditions under which defence lawyers are permitted to see their clients. They may see them only on the family visiting day, which shortens the family visit; they are regularly searched and not permitted to take notes. The Minister of Interior has promised to rectify these matters.

Amnesty International still receives reports of torture and ill-treatment of political prisoners. In 1977 the organization initiated 16 telegram campaigns on behalf of political prisoners, who had either disappeared after arrest, were in need of immediate medical attention, or had been tortured. In the past year Amnesty International heard of the cases of three prisoners, Pablo Pietrafesa, Pedro Benitez and Juan Luis Lopez Estigarribia, who were released because of their physical condition as a result of torture. A number of people have reported that some of the 19 trade unionists arrested in December 1977 were ill-treated during the first few days of detention.

In the leaflet *Deaths under Torture and Disappearances*, published in October 1977, Amnesty International called on the public to write letters to the President of Paraguay, requesting a public investigation into the deaths under torture or disappearances of 36 political prisoners.

Number of Prisoners

At the height of the last wave of repressive measures (April-June 1976), the estimated number of political prisoners was about 1,000. In the following year this figure declined to about 300-400. Amnesty International estimates there are now 200-250 political prisoners. Due to the failure of the Paraguayan authorities to provide official information on detainees, numbers are inevitably always approximate.

Government

During 1977 an elected 60-member Constitutional Convention, made up of an overwhelming majority of Colorado Party members, revised Article 173 of the 1967 Constitution enabling the President, General Stroessner, to stand for a further term in the February 1978 elections. General Stroessner, supported by the Colorado Party and the armed forces, was re-elected by large majorities in 1958, 1963, 1968 and 1973. The legal opposition parties refused to participate in the Constitutional Convention because the revision of the 1967 Constitution would endanger their chance of securing a majority of votes in the 1978 elections.

Opposition parties in Paraguay are strictly limited: the Communist Party has been outlawed and the Christian Democrat Party was not registered by the Electoral Commission for the February elections. Because of the restrictions—and in an attempt to avoid vote splitting—the Liberal Radical Party and the Liberal Party joined forces under the name of the United Liberal Party. Realizing the threat that this alliance would pose at election time, the Government reacted by recognizing only small factions of the two original parties to be registered by the Electoral Commission as the true opposition parties. Consequently, the attempted party unification proved counter-productive and left broad sectors of the original parties without either a place in the ballot or a party newspaper. The Liberal Radical Party group, led by Domingo Laino, the Febrerista Party and the Christian Democrat Party all advised that their supporters' vote should be a blank ballot.

On 12 February 1978, General Alfredo Stroessner was re-elected for his sixth term as President of Paraguay by obtaining just under 90% of the votes cast: the Government reported that he received 890,361 votes. There were 180,000 abstentions. The Colorado Party kept the two-thirds majority in the Congress which they have maintained since 1947.

AMNESTY INTERNATIONAL is a worldwide human rights movement which is independent of any government, political faction, ideology, economic interest or religious creed. It works for the release of men and women imprisoned anywhere for their beliefs, colour, ethnic origin, sex, language or religion, provided they have neither used nor advocated violence. These are termed "prisoners of conscience".

AMNESTY INTERNATIONAL opposes torture and the death penalty in all cases and without reservation. It advocates fair and early trials for all political prisoners and works on behalf of persons detained without charge or without trial and those detained after expiry of their sentences.

AMNESTY INTERNATIONAL seeks observance throughout the world of the United Nations Universal Declaration of Human Rights and the UN Standard Minimum Rules for the Treatment of Prisoners.

AMNESTY INTERNATIONAL has 2,000 adoption groups and national sections in 35 countries in Africa, Asia, Europe, the Middle East, North America and Latin America and individual members in a further 74 countries. Each adoption group works for at least two prisoners of conscience in countries other than its own. These countries are balanced geographically and politically to ensure impartiality. Information about prisoners and human rights violations emanates from Amnesty International's Research Department in London.

AMNESTY INTERNATIONAL has consultative status with the United Nations (ECOSOC), UNESCO and the Council of Europe, has cooperative relations with the Inter-American Commission on Human Rights of the Organization of American States, and has observer status with the Organization of African Unity (Bureau for the Placement and Education of African Refugees).

AMNESTY INTERNATIONAL is financed by subscriptions and donations of its worldwide membership. To safeguard the independence of the organization, all contributions are strictly controlled by guidelines laid down by AI's International Council, and income and expenditure are made public in an annual financial report.

Briefing Paper Number 4

ISBN 0 900058 33 1
First published July 1976
Second impression May 1978
AI Index: PUB 48/00/76
Published by Amne
10 Southampton S
Printed in Great B

Amnesty Interna
inclusive for 10 i
(US 50 cents) for